FOREX T SYSTEM: STRATEGIES OF FOREX TRADING REVEALED

Simple and Easy Strategy on How to Make Good Profits in Forex Trading

By: Steven S. Finley

FOREX TRADING SYSTEM

TABLE OF CONTENTS

Table of Contents 2

Publisher's Notes 3

Dedication 4

Chapter 1- Difference between the STOCK market and the FOREX market 5

Chapter 2- 12 Most Common Trading Terms You Must Know .. 10

Chapter 3- 6 Useful Concepts in FOREX Market 14

Chapter 4- Primary Tools for Technical Analysis 20

Chapter 5- Two Main Essential Categories of Strategy 35

Chapter 6- Understanding the Fundamentals of Risk Management 37

Chapter 7- 5 Fundamental Methods on How To Become Part of the 10% That WIN! 40

Chapter 8- Conclusion 44

About The Author 46

Steven S. Finley

PUBLISHER'S NOTES
Disclaimer

This publication is intended to provide basic information. No action should be taken solely on the contents of this book.

The author and publisher specifically disclaim all responsibility for any liability, loss or risk, personal or otherwise, which is incurred as a consequence, directly or indirectly, from the use or application of any contents of this book.

Any and all product names referenced within this book are the trademarks of their respective owners. None of these owners have sponsored, authorized, endorsed, or approved this book.

Always read all information provided by the manufacturers' product labels before using their products. The author and publisher are not responsible for claims made by manufacturers.

Paperback Edition
Speedy Publishing, LLC
40 E. Main Street, #1156
Newark, DE 19711
This book is a reprint.

Manufactured in the United States of America

Dedication

Secret, Strategies in Forex Trading are very interesting. This book can provide information that every reader needs. That's why I dedicate this to those who are determined to make good profits in Forex Trading.

Steven S. Finley

Chapter 1 - Difference between the STOCK market and the FOREX market

In this chapter, I will discuss the general definitions of the Stock Market and the Forex Market. And the significant differences between the two as well as the pros and cons of each.

What is the Stock Market?

The definition of the stock market is simply the business of buying and selling stock for the financial aspect. Stock refers to a supply of money that a company has raised. Investors (or stockholders) give the company this supply of money in order to help that company grow, therefore increasing the value of their stock and in turn making a profit.

The stock market is one of the more traditional ways to create a profit from an investment… even without having much knowledge about it. A person with little or no experience can make a few bucks without much research with traditional investments, such as stocks, bonds and blue chips.

But with thousands of companies to choose from, it can be quite overwhelming… and you never know when a company will go bankrupt or fold altogether.

There can be a lot of risk and uncertainty when going after large gains in short amounts of time. It can be difficult to develop a system that can provide a consistent 10 to 15% profit on a yearly basis.

The stock market is country specific, and deals only in business and currencies within that region. There are set business hours that typically follow the more traditional business day, and is closed on Holidays and weekends.

Let's check out the forex market...

The Definition of the Forex Market

The forex market, also known as the foreign exchange or the fx market, is the place where currencies are traded. It is the largest, most liquid market in the world with an average traded value of over 4 trillion per day and includes all of the currencies in the world.

Compare that to the $25 billion per day that the New York Stock Exchange trades and you can easily see how enormous the forex market really is. It actually equates to more than 3 times the total amount of stocks and futures markets combined. Forex is awesome!

What exactly is traded on the forex market you ask? The simple answer is money. It is the simultaneous buying of one currency and the selling of another. Currencies are traded through a broker and are always traded in pairs.

EXAMPLE: The euro and the US dollar (EUR/USD)

-OR-

The British Pound and the Japanese Yen
(GBP/JPY)

Confused? Think of it as buying a traditional 'share' in a particular country. Let's say you buy British Pound, you are essentially buying a share in the British economy as the price of the GBP is a direct reflection of what the market thinks about not only the current, but the future health of the British economy.

Market Hours

Unlike the traditional stock market, the forex market is open 24 hours a day. At any time, somewhere around the world, a financial center is open for business and is exchanging currencies every hour of the day and night.

It follows the sun around the world, so you can trade late at night or early in the morning.

TIME ZONE	NEW YORK	GMT
Tokyo Open	7:00 p.m.	0.00
Tokyo Close	4:00 a.m.	9:00
London Open	3:00 a.m.	8:00
London Close	12:00 p.m.	17:00
New York Open	8:00 a.m.	13:00
New York Close	5:00 p.m.	22:00

Keep in mind that these additional hours also add additional risk for us since we aren't able to monitor our investments 24 hours every day. There are several safety options, such as limit that we will discuss in another chapter.

FOREX TRADING SYSTEM
Forex Trading In Multiple Currencies

One of the most critical things that you must understand in forex trading is hour to correctly determine the value of multiple currencies.

Obviously not everyone will trade in US dollars.

But with so many variables, how can you tell a good buy or sell without complete understanding of the value of foreign currencies?

Your first step is to figure out the current exchange rate between the currencies in question. I highly recommend using this free currency converter:

Http://www.oanda.com

They are very reliable and have tons of information to help you as well. Aside from the information that I am giving you here, I highly recommend you study the materials available on their website as well.

Keep in mind that these currency converters will not be consistently accurate down to the cent or fraction of a particular currency at all times throughout any day, but it will give you a solid starting point.

Currency conversion is usually expressed in a ratio known as the cross rate. Normally you will see them listed in pairs in an xxx/yyy manner, with the xxx referred to as the 'base' currency (or home currency).

The base currency is usually always listed as a whole number, while the converted currency will be expressed with a decimal that is as close as possible to the base rate.

> **EXAMPLE:** 1 US dollar = 0.61484 British Pound
>
> -OR-
>
> 1.000 USD/0.61484 GBP

You'll notice that the base currency is almost always in single units (such as one dollar instead of ten). And since the whole number (often referred to as the 'big' figure) of the secondary currency almost never changes, it is usually only referred to as the decimal point.

Also with the consolidation of most of the European market using the Euro, many currencies such as franc or the lira have been eliminated, making trading currencies much less complicated.

It will take a bit of time, but once you get used to the base values of each currency, the changes will become more obvious to you, therefore making it easier and less confusing to monitor and you'll be making profitable trading decisions right along with the pros.

Chapter 2 - 12 Most Common Trading Terms You Must Know

Now you most likely won't be standing amidst a few hundred other screaming stockbrokers on Wall Street, but it is important that you understand some of the terms that you would be hearing if you were. You want to be sure to understand what these terms mean in your trading.

These are some of the most common Trading terms:

• **Bid/ask spread** – also known as the bid/offer spread, is the quote of the price at which the parties involved are willing to buy or sell. The bid price is the price that a party is willing to purchase. While asking or offer price is the price at which the party is willing to sell the same. The difference between the two prices is considered the spread.

If the spread cannot be closed, then no deal can be made. The forward price (or agreed upon price) and all details involved in the transaction are written in a contract and referred to as forward points. Most of the time it is outlined as available until a certain date and if this transaction isn't completed by that date (transaction date), and then at that time it must be renegotiated.

• **Currency Pair** – since the value of one currency is only relevant when put in terms of another, forex traders will always deal in currency pairs.

As I mentioned before, the first currency in the pair considers the 'base' currency. The second currency in the pair is the 'counter' currency.

• **_Leverage & Margin_** – Margin is a good faith deposit that a trader puts up as collateral to hold a position. The amount of margin that a trader puts up determines his leverage.

In other words, when a trader opens a position larger than the amount of funds required opening it, the trader has put down margin to receive leverage.

While margin refers to the amount of funds a trader has put down as collateral, leverage refers to the amount of money he controls relative to the margin.

• **_Pip_** – (Percentage in Point) refers to the very last digit of a currency price.

Just for illustrative purposes, let's take the Euro/USD at 1.2635. If the sell price was 1.2638 then we have a 3 pip increase. Should the Euro/USD sell at 1.3635 then we have a 100 pip increase.

• **_Stop_** – Limit Order – An order to buy or sell a certain quantity of a certain security at a specified price or better, but only after a specified price has been reached. A stop limit order is essentially a combination of a stop order and a limit order.

- **Rollover/ Carry Trade** – A popular trading strategy used in the forex market. It guarantees traders at least some return on their medium and longer term positions.

In the carry trade, speculators buy high interest currencies and sell currencies with low interest rates. These positions ensure that each trading day rollover- interest will be posted to the traders account. It has the potential to significantly enhance a return.

Rollover is also sometimes referred to reinvesting any earnings in additional stock or currencies.

- **Bear Market** – Refers to a strong trend of downward movement in several areas of the market.

- **Bull Market** – Refers to a strong upward trend in several areas of the market.

- **Open Order** – Your order remains pending until it is either executed or cancelled.

- **Stop Order** – Cancels any pending orders that are placed with the broker.

- **Market Makers/Jobbers** – Stockbrokers who hold or purchase securities at low prices for the purpose of selling them to traders in a higher priced market so that the trader can turn around and resell them for a profit... essentially creating a separate market are called market makers (also known as jobbers in Britain).

- **Whipsaw** – A term for what happens when the market trends point toward a specific direction, causing a buy or sell and then the opposite effect occurs.

This will happen occasionally and you realistically cannot expect to win with every purchase. My best advice when it happens is to wait it out. The market will rebound and you can still make a profit or at least break even, if you are patient.

Those are just some of the most commonly used terms that I wanted you to be familiar with. It should help you to understand a bit about the market lingo before we get into the meat of the course, where you will learn the details of many of the terms above.

Chapter 3- 6 Useful Concepts in Forex Market

The forex market is by far the biggest and most popular financial market in the world. It is traded globally by individuals as well as banks and large organizations.

The chart below shows the global foreign exchange activity, with the United States dollar (USD) being the most traded currencies, with the Euro share at 2nd and the Japanese yen at 3rd.

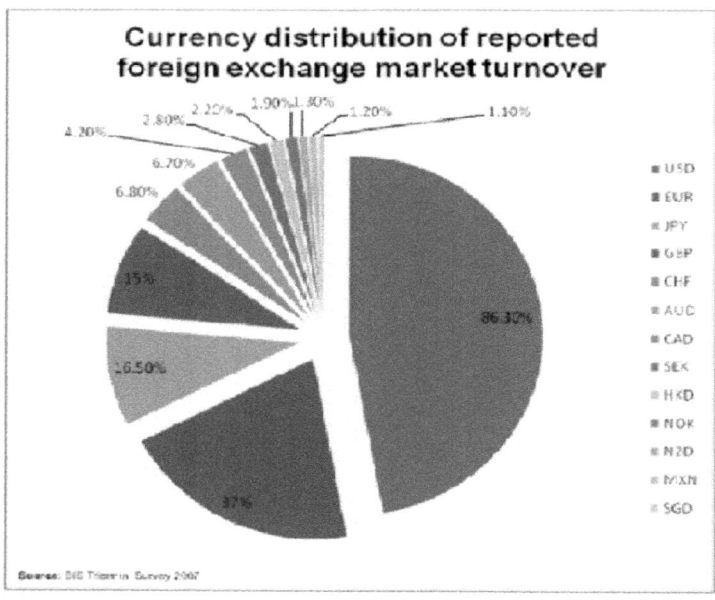

Steven S. Finley
The Nature of the Forex Market

The forex market is an over the counter market, which simply means that there is no central exchange or clearing house where orders are matched and transactions occur.

Large commercial banks trade with each other through what's known as the Electronic Brokerage System (EBS). Such banks will only make their quotes available to other banks with which they trade. This market is not accessible to individual or retail traders.

Then there are the online market makers. This is where individual traders can access the forex market through online market makers that primarily trade out of the US and the UK.

Forex: Past & Present

Until the late 1990's the forex market was really only available to the 'BIG Players'. You could basically only trade if you had at least $10 million to start with!

It was originally intended to be used by bankers and large institutions- not by us 'little' guys.

Because of the rise of the internet, online forex trading firms are now able to offer trading account to normal folks like us.

Now all you need to trade in the forex market is a computer, a high speed internet connection and this guide.

Financial Markets

Here is a simple comparison table of various financial markets and some of their basic features:

	Equities	Futures	Forex
Market Structure	Over the Counter (OTC) or Exchanged Traded, with Electronic Communication Network (ECN) routing available for both.	Exchanged Traded through open outcry in trading pits; some contracts are traded by ECN after hours.	Over the Counter (OTC) market with access to price determined by the market maker.
Spreads	Spreads fluctuate according to demand and supply.	Spreads fluctuate according to demand and supply.	Spreads fluctuate according to demand and supply.
Execution	Orders on listed stocks are placed with a specialist, who matches buyers and sellers, providing liquidity from his own account as well. OTC orders can be sent to market makers who take the opposite side of the trade at their quoted side.	Orders are executed via open outcry at the exchange pit for each future contract. Orders entered electronically are routed to the pits to be executed.	Orders on the Inter-bank market are sent directly to the counter party via Reuters or EBS. Orders executed with online market makers are executed at the market maker with the market maker as the counter party.
Trading Hours	Typically 9:30am to 4:00pm local time. Off-hours trading can	Vary by product, usually starts from 9:00am to 3:00pm local time. Off-hours trading is possible, but illiquid.	Market, Stop, Stop-limit, Limit

	occur through ECN's but it is illiquid.		
Volume	Available	Available	Not Available
Market Size	100-200 billion USD daily volumes in the US.	300-500 billion USD daily volumes in the US.	1.5 trillion daily volume worldwide.
Transaction Cost	Spread and commission/service charge.	Spread and commission/service	

What is a 'Spread"?

We've already defined the spread to mean the difference between the bid price and the ask price, which constitutes the cost of the trade. In fact, all trades have spread... stocks, futures, commodities, etc.

Be aware that many online trading firms like to promote margin forex trading as virtually cost free – commission free, no service charge, no hidden cost, etc.

The spread IS the cost of trading AND is also the main source of revenue for the trading firms.

The spread may seem to be a small expense, but once you add up all the costs of all the trades, it can eat up your share of the profits pretty darn fast!

On the other hand, while you want to find the tightest spread possible, anything that is far lower than typical is skeptical. Since the spread is the main source of revenue for the trading firm, if the firm doesn't earn enough from it there may be any other hidden costs involved in the transaction.

FOREX TRADING SYSTEM
Different Types of Orders

The following are some of the different types of orders available that can help you to protect yourself in your trading ventures. This isn't all that are available, but just some of the basic orders for you to make the most out of. Use them wisely!

- **Market Orders** – a buy or sell order in which the forex firm is to execute the order at the best available current price.

- **GTC** – (Good Until Cancelled) An order will be valid until it is cancelled, regardless of the trading session. (Generally, the entry orders, stop loss orders and take profit orders are all GTC orders in online forex trading).

- **Entry Orders** – A request from a trader to a forex firm to buy or sell a specified amount of a particular currency pair at a specific price. The order will be filled once the requested price is met.

- **Take Profit Orders** – An order placed to close a position when it reaches a specified price. It is designed to limit a trader's loss on a given position. This is how it works… if the position is opened by buying a currency pair, the stop loss order would be a request to sell the position when the price fell to a specified level and vice versa.

Traders are strongly recommended to use stop loss orders to limit their losses. It is also important to use stop loss orders when investors may enter a situation where they are unable to monitor their portfolios for an extended period of time.

How To Use Margins

A margin account allows customers to open positions with a higher value than the amount of funds they have deposited in their account.

Also known as trading on a leveraged basis, most online firms offer up to 200 times leverage on a mini contract account. The forex market offers the highest leverage among other trading instruments with a margin requirement of 0.5% for open positions.

The equity in excess of the margin requirement acts as a cushion for the trader. If a trader loses on a position to the point that the cushion runs out, then a margin call will result.

The trader must then deposit more funds before the margin call or the position will be closed. The account will be 'margined out', meaning that all positions will be closed, once the equity falls below the margin requirement.

Most trading firms offer customizable leverage; traders can choose the leverage ratio that they feel most comfortable with. Be aware of how to guard against over trading an account and managing overall risk – we will cover that more in chapter 6.

Chapter 4- Primary Tools for Technical Analysis

Fundamental analysis and technical analysis are the two major approaches to analyzing and studying the currency market, the first focusing on the underlying causes of the price movements... such as economic, social and political forces that drive supply and demand.

Technical analysis focuses on the studies of the price movements themselves.

I believe that the premise of technical analysis is that all current market information is already reflected in the price movement which is why we will focus on the latter.

In the following chapter I will explain briefly the primary tools used for technical analysis, arming you with the knowledge of the professionals. Use this to compare notes and ideas, suggestions and advice with your trading firm.

Let's get to it.

Using Charts

Charts are the most important tool in your understanding of the total sum of what is happening in the market. It is simply a visualized representation of the price movements... a reflection of the psychology of the market and a visualization of the interaction between buyers and

Steven S. Finley

sellers, and shows how the market values a particular asset based on the information available.

Because of this, it is considered to be an indispensable tool in the arsenal of any trader.

There are 3 major charts: bar charts, candlestick charts and line charts.

We will get into a bit more detail with the Candlestick charts a bit later, since they are the most commonly used charts amongst active traders.

1. Bar Charts – Bar charts provide traders with 4 key pieces of information for a given time frame:
- The opening price during that time frame
- The closing price
- The high price
- The low price

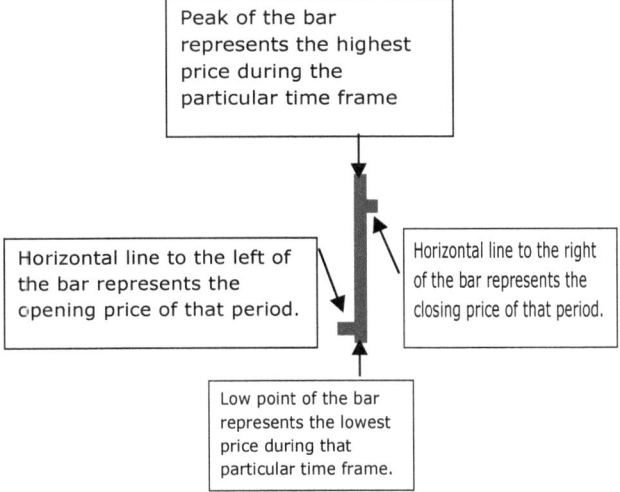

Bar charts can be applied to all time frames and therefore, a single bar can summarize price activity over the past minute or

A good rule of thumb is that the longer the time frame, the more significant it is since it will account for more data and will be a better reflection of the market's psychological.

3. Candlestick Charts – Just like the bar chart, a candlestick chart contains the markets open, closing, low and high price points of a specific time frame. The main difference being that the candlestick's body will show the range between the opening price and the closing price during that particular time frame.

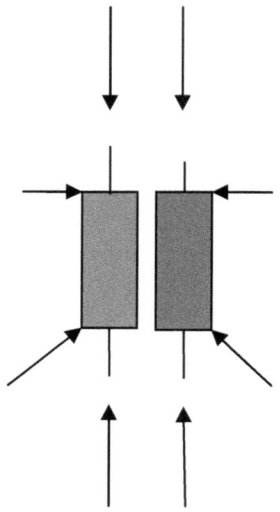

Candlestick charts are more popular than the bar charts or line charts since they are more visually appealing and helps to identify more information. (See the intro to candlestick for more information).

2. Line Charts – These present much less information than the previous types of charts. They only show the closing price for a series of periods, therefore serve best to measure the overall direction of long-term trends.

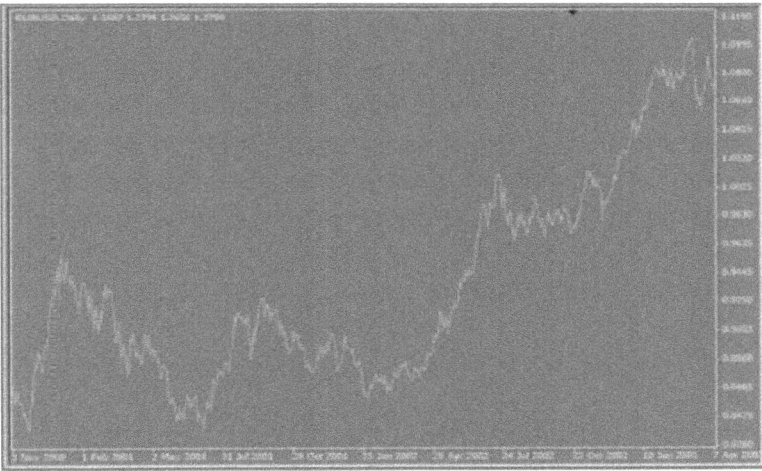

Line Charts are of limited use for most traders, but will show simply and clearly the direction of the trend which can be extremely useful.

Support & Resistance

Support levels are prices where buyers have shown or are likely to show strength.

Resistance levels are prices where sellers are likely to be strong.

Support levels are basically giving the market a 'floor', since this is the area in which buyers tend to be strong. If the current price is at a strong support level, then traders can expect buyers to step in and drive the price up – or at least keep it from moving any lower.

Resistance levels basically perform the exact opposite, and are essentially a 'ceiling' to the market. If the price is at or raises to a strong resistance level, then sellers in short term positions may enter the market while sellers in long positions may cover their positions to take their profits.

Many times when a price breaks through a resistance level, it will trigger a large number of stop orders and thereby greatly increases buying power. Be careful here though, since not every breakout is valid. The same dangers of false breakouts apply to support levels as well.

Identifying the Trends

A trend simply represents a general direction of a market.

There is a physical law stating that an object in motion tends to continue in that motion until some extreme force causes it to change direction. Price trends are no different. A strong price trend will continue in its current direction unless there is a price reversal indication, that will show up in your technical analysis – or even in fundamental analysis.

There are 3 phases of major trends that you should be aware of in your analysis; Accumulation, public participation and distribution.

Steven S. Finley

The accumulation phase is the first part of the trend which represents those who are well informed that will buy or sell.

Meaning simply that if the well informed or more seasoned, experienced traders recognize that a current downward trend is coming to an end, then they would buy – and vice versa.

The public participation is essentially when the masses would recognize the same and follow suit.

The third and final phase – the distribution phase – occurs when everyone else catches on and public participation increases even further. It is at this point that the well informed, seasoned investors who accumulated during the accumulation phase would begin to sell, or vice versa.

Highs & Lows

As a general rule of thumb, the existence of a trend depends on a series of highs and lows. 2 consecutive highs, each above the previous relative high and 2 relative lows above the previous low would constitute a tentative uptrend. A 3rd relative high would confirm that trend.

It is very important to keep in mind that markets do not always move in trends!

They also spend a lot of time in 'ranges' fluctuating between already established highs and lows. A range bound market is often referred to as a 'sideways' market since it is neither moving in an upward trend or a downward trend.

The price during a sideways market is often simply building support for a continued move in the original direction.

Drawing Trend Lines

Trend lines are drawn on historical price levels that show the general direction of where the market is heading and also provides indications of support or resistance.

Drawing trend lines is a highly subjective matter, due to the fact that there are so many variables.

How it works is this… In an uptrend a trend line should connect the relative low points on the chart. The line connecting the lows in a long term position will be a support line that can provide a floor for partial retracements. The downtrend line that connects the relative highs on the chart will similarly act as resistance to shorter moves back higher.

It is important to be flexible when drawing trend lines and redraw trend lines whenever necessary.

How to Use Price Channels

In a trending market, a price channel can often be drawn between two parallel support and resistance levels. The key to this price channel is that the lines be drawn parallel to each other and the value of the price channel depends on that.

Unlike trend lines, price channels should not be forced on a chart where they are not quickly apparent.

Steven S. Finley

How it works is this... once a trend line is established, draw a duplicate line parallel on the chart. Then move it up to the relative highs above or down to the relative lows below the trend line.

If two or more fit with the line, then you may have located a valid price channel. Otherwise the market may be too volatile – even in the middle of a strong trend, to plot a price channel.

Intro to Candlestick

Candlestick charts contain the markets open, closing, low and highs of a specific time frame.

On a daily chart, each candle represents a 24 hour period and contains the information indicated above. On an hourly chart, each candle represents an hour... and so on.

But since the forex market never opens and closes, how can there be an open and closing price? To identify this information, the chart provider will decide on a time, say 5 PM EST, as the daily open and closing time.

Keep in mind that different chart providers may have different opening and closing times and traders may notice that the charts may differ from different providers.

Chart Patterns & What They Mean To You

There are recurring patterns on these candlestick charts that can be observed by technical analysis. These patterns are like recurring pictures that tend to occur when a trend is starting or about to end, or even reverse its direction.

FOREX TRADING SYSTEM

They provide an excellent visualization of the price movements and can give us a good idea of what is happening in the market.

These patterns are the best gage for identifying trends in the market.

> **EXAMPLE:** If a candlestick is very short, it implies that the range for trading that day was very tight. If this candle appears after a strong uptrend, it may suggest that sellers are beginning to enter the market more aggressively and thus the price may be on its way back down.

Eventually, with a bit of practice, these candlesticks

Patterns can be easily used to identify potential trends in the market – especially when used in conjunction with other indicators, allowing you to enter the market with strong references to the patters.

Here are some key patterns to watch out for:

Doji/Double Doji...

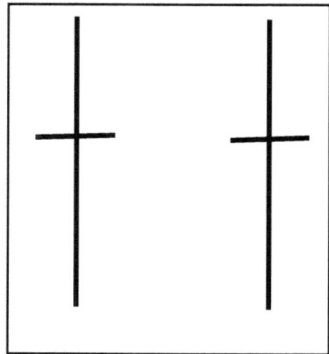

Steven S. Finley

This pattern indicates indecision in the marketplace as the price has a big range but isn't going anywhere.

Hammer – Hanging Men...

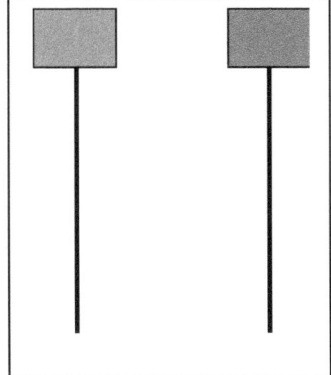

This is an indication of a good reversal pattern after a severe trend. It signifies a weakening market. The pattern is considered a hammer after a downturn and a hanging man after an uptrend.

Evening Star

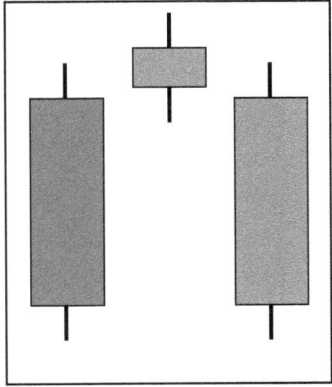

FOREX TRADING SYSTEM

The reversal pattern shows trend changes direction after making new highs.

Morning Star...

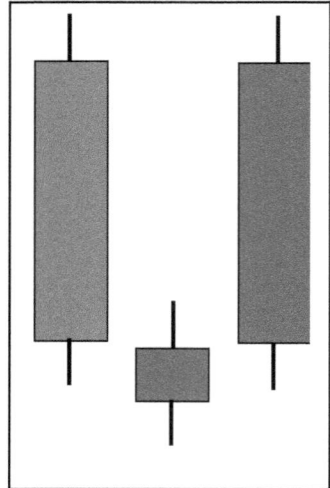

Opposite of the evening star – reversal pattern shows trend changes direction after making new lows.

Bear Market...

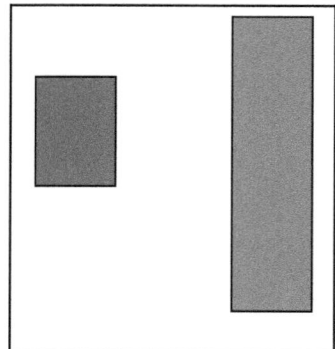

Steven S. Finley
Common pattern after strong up trends. Signifies that buyers are losing control.

Bull Market

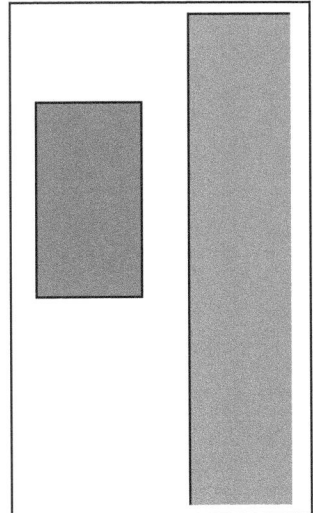

Common pattern after dramatic downtrends. Signifies that downtrend has lost momentum.

Harami...

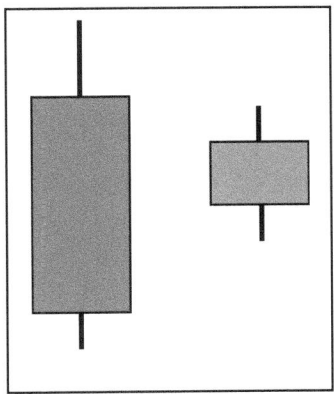

Harami shows a trend that is losing momentum and may reverse.

Shooting Star...

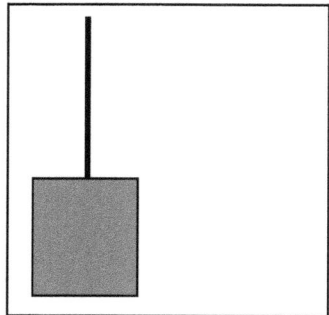

Reversal patterns that occur after gaps. Buyers may make new highs but fail to sustain them.

Piercing Line...

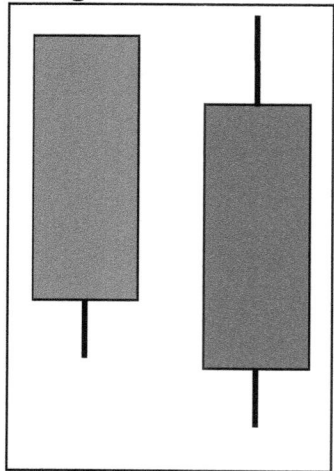

A bullish reversal pattern which shows sellers are losing their dominance.

Dark Cloud Cover...

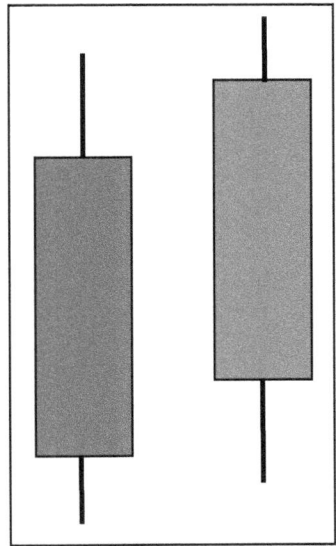

The bearish pattern showing slowing buyer momentum.

Keep in mind that you will recognize these patterns as you gain more experience. These are just some of the patterns to watch out for.

Using Fibonacci Retracements

Fibonacci retracements are based on mathematical numbers that repeat themselves and attempt to measure the likely points that a currency pair will retrace, or pull back to within a range.

Now, while I'm not about to get into the mathematical system that is used (Boring!) I will let you know that you can use

FOREX TRADING SYSTEM

charting software with the Fibonacci function, or simply let you forex firm help with your charting.

Also, note that Fibonacci retracements can be used in both bull (uptrend) and bear (downtrend) markets. You will need to look for retracement levels and use them with your candlestick patterns to confirm your trades.

Technical Indicators

Based on different mathematical calculations, technical indicators are statistics of past market data. Traders use them extensively in their technical analysis to predict currency trends.

The two major technical indicators are:

Trend following indicators reflect the direction and the strength of a current trend. Traders may enter a position when the trend following indicators are showing the current trend in a strong momentum in either direction.

The most common trend following indicators is moving averages and Bollinger bands.

Oscillators are indicators banded between two extreme values that reflect short term overbought or oversold conditions. The most common oscillators are RSI (relative strength index), MACD (moving average convergence difference) and stochastic.

Most charting packages usually include the common technical indicators or you can find a charting package and add the indicators that you want if they aren't included.

You will probably use a mix between the trend following indicators and the oscillators. Use whatever you are comfortable with.

Chapter 5 - Two Main Essential Categories of Strategy

Now that you understand a bit more about how the forex market works, you need to determine your trading strategy. There really is only one method... trial and error.

I can suggest to you to open up a Demo account (there are many available) although I believe that it makes a huge difference when using real money. So open up a demo account if you wish, but use it to learn the terms and such – then tries it for real. Remember, slow and steady wins the race!

The truth be told, almost any proven forex strategy does have the potential for profit. Some have a greater potential for profit, but also carry higher risk, and vice versa.

Every strategy can be put into one of two main categories... long term or short term.

The Long & Short of it

Basically self explanatory, long or short positions are essentially that, the truth being, that you could even incorporate both types into your strategy.

Short term forex strategies tend to carry more potential for greater profits. That being said, they also carry greater potential for substantial risks. They also require vigilance... you must be watching the market constantly, so that you are able to pick out the best times to buy or sell, as well as placing specific orders.

Now on the other end of the stick, **long term** positions tend to be more stable, as well as significantly less risky, thus aren't usually as quick to produce substantial profits. But you are able to ride out any small fluctuations and wait to buy or sell until the time is right.

Furthermore, long positions are more leisurely and require a lot less attention. It is a personal preference and my best advice is to try them both and see what works best for you. You may decide to do both and that's okay too!

Steven S. Finley

Chapter 6- Understanding the Fundamentals of Risk Management

Hopefully now you understand that the forex market behaves a bit different than other markets. Currency markets are highly speculative and volatile in nature.

Any currency can become very expensive or very cheap in a matter of days, hours or sometimes even minutes.

The unpredictable nature of this market is one of the things that attract traders to the currency market.

With that being said money management is critical and makes the difference between the winners and the losers.

Money Management

Money management is the most significant part of any trading system. Most traders don't understand how important it really is.

It is important to understand the concept of money management and to understand the difference between it and trading decisions. Money management represents the amount of money that you are going to put on one trade and the risk you are going to accept for this trade.

First of all, your risk per trade should never exceed 3% per trade. It is better to adjust your risk to 1% or 2%, but if you are confident in your trading system then you can adjust it up to 3%.

Secondly, adjust your stop loss so that you never lost more than you are comfortable with on a single trade.

Now you also want to make sure that you diversify your trades between several currencies and not trade just one pair. It is also important that you diversify your orders between currencies that have low correlation.

There are many different money management strategies. It is critical that you adopt the strategies that work for you and use them diligently to help manage your risk.

Using Limit Orders

We understand that forex markets can be volatile and difficult to predict. While limiting the impact of any adverse price movements, using limit orders can help you capitalize on short term price movements.

A limit order is simply a standard amount at which you have instructed your forex firm to buy or sell a position. Setting these limits, protects you and your investments.

While there are no guarantees that the use of these types of orders will limit your losses and protect your profits in all market conditions, a disciplined use of market orders will help you reduce the risk that you are taking. It will also give you peace of mind in your trading.

We've covered many of the market orders that are available in the forex market. However, keep in mind that not all market orders are available at all online forex brokers.

Steven S. Finley

So when you open your account with a broker or forex firm, make sure the orders that you want to use are available..

Chapter 7 - 5 Fundamental Methods on How To Become Part of the 10% That WIN!

Why do traders lose? The statistics show that 90% of all traders lose money.

It's an age old question and while there is no magic formula and no way that anyone can guarantee that you won't lose money, there are 5 fundamental things that you can do to become part of the 10% THAT ARE CONSISTENTLY PROFITABLE.

How do you do that?

1.   Develop a clear and concise method.

First of all, if your goal is to become a consistently successful trader, you must have a clear and concise method for trading.

In order to have that you must have a clear and precise way of looking at and reading the markets. Guessing or going by gut instinct might work occasionally, but if you don't have a specific method, then you don't have a way to know what constitutes a buy or sell signal, and aren't able to correctly identify the trend.

The way to go about this is to write it down. You need to define in writing what your analytical tools are and how to use them. It really doesn't matter what charts you use as long you actually take the effort to define it.

In other words, for example:

- What constitutes a buy
- What constitutes a sell
- What constitutes a stop
- Instructions on exiting a position
- When to use limit orders

Clearly define your methods and define it by writing it down, and keep it simple! Don't make it too complicated… if you can't write it on the back of your hand it's probably too complicated.

2. You must have the discipline to follow that method.

Once you have clearly and concisely defined your methodology, you absolutely must have the discipline to follow through with that method.
If you view a price chart different than you did 2 months ago then you either haven't developed your method, or you lack the discipline to follow it.
The formula for success is to consistently follow and apply a proven method.

3. Have realistic expectations

Don't be greedy!
We've all seen the ads that may get our blood pumping with promises of becoming wealthy overnight while we sleep, or investing a few bucks in stock and making a million in a week, what usually sounds too good to be true usually is.

Now it is possible to experience above average returns or some trades, although it may be difficult to do without above average risk.

The goal for every trader, especially in the first year is to not lose money! Any percent return you see above that is icing on the cake.

In other words, don't allow yourself to get greedy! This is the downfall of many traders. They start to feel overly confident and start taking higher risks and end up losing much cash!

4.   Be Patient

One of the reasons that most of us get into trading and the forex market is because it's exciting. I mean, let's face it, trading is a lot like gambling and anytime money is involved, it tends to get our blood pumping.

As a result, you will get tempted to start taking shortcuts on your methods or you'll start making trades of lesser and lesser quality, seriously adding to your levels of risk and inherently over trading!

I have found that by reminding myself that I have no reason to worry about missing that next great opportunity, because there is another one right around the corner... guaranteed.

5.   Manage Your Risk by Managing Your Money

I could seriously write a whole book on the importance of managing your money. There are so many factors in managing your money... such as risk/reward analysis, probability of success and failure, and so much more.

With that in mind, I am going to address the issue of money management with a focus on risk on the entire portfolio size and not each individual transaction. You'll see what I mean.

Steven S. Finley

I believe that many traders tend to be over aggressive in their trades. A good rule of thumb is to never risk any higher that 1-3% of your portfolio. If you have a small trading account, then trade small.

The bottom line to becoming a consistently successful trader is longevity! Keep your risks small and you'll be able to weather the rough spots. If you're risking 25% of your portfolio on each trade, then it will only take 4 consecutive losses for you to be completely out of business.

Remember the story of the tortoise and the hare… slow and steady win the race!

Although it is my belief that making money in the foreign exchange market is easier than any of the other trading markets, it isn't easily done without your eyes wide open.

I can guarantee if you practice the above 5 steps, you won't be caught in the 90% of losing traders.

Let's wrap this up….

Chapter 8- Conclusion

Let's recap:
• The forex market represents the electronic over-the-counter markets where currencies are traded worldwide 24 hours a day, five and a half days a week. The typical means of trading forex are on the spot, futures and forwards markets.

• Currencies are "priced" in currency pairs and are quoted either directly or indirectly.

• Currencies typically have two prices: bid (the amount that the market will buy the quote currency for in relation to the base currency); and ask (the amount the market will sell one unit of the base currency for in relation to the quote currency). The bid price is always smaller than the ask price.

• Unlike conventional equity and debt markets, forex investors have access to large amounts of leverage, which allows substantial positions to be taken without making a large initial investment.

• The adoption and elimination of several global currency systems over time led to the formation of the present currency exchange system, in which most countries use some measure of floating exchange rates.

• Governments, central banks, banks and other financial institutions, hedgers, and speculators are the main players in the forex market.

• The main economic theories found in the foreign exchange deal with parity conditions such as those involving interest rates and inflation. Overall, a country's qualitative and quantitative factors are seen as large influences on its currency in the forex market.

Steven S. Finley

• Forex traders use fundamental analysis to view currencies and their countries like companies, thereby using economic announcements to gain an idea of the currency's true value.

• Forex traders use technical analysis to look at currencies the same way they would any other asset and, therefore, uses technical tools such as trends, charts and indicators in their trading strategies.

• Unlike stock trades, forex traders have minimal commissions and related fees. But new forex traders should take a conservative approach and use orders, such as the take-profit or stop-loss, to minimize losses.

Just keep in mind that managing your money goes hand in hand with managing your risks, which is the key to any kind of investment… and remember to not be greedy. Slow and steady wins the race every time.

To Your Success!

About The Author

Steven S. Finley, shares his vast knowledge and experience in SECRET STRATEGIES OF FOREX TRADING REVEALED. . He is best known for tracing the natural Fibonacci movements in the market that help traders turn patterns into profit. Steven has mentored thousands of traders, from novices to experts.

Lightning Source UK Ltd.
Milton Keynes UK
UKHW020634291121
394768UK00005B/315